downtownDIY

Sewing

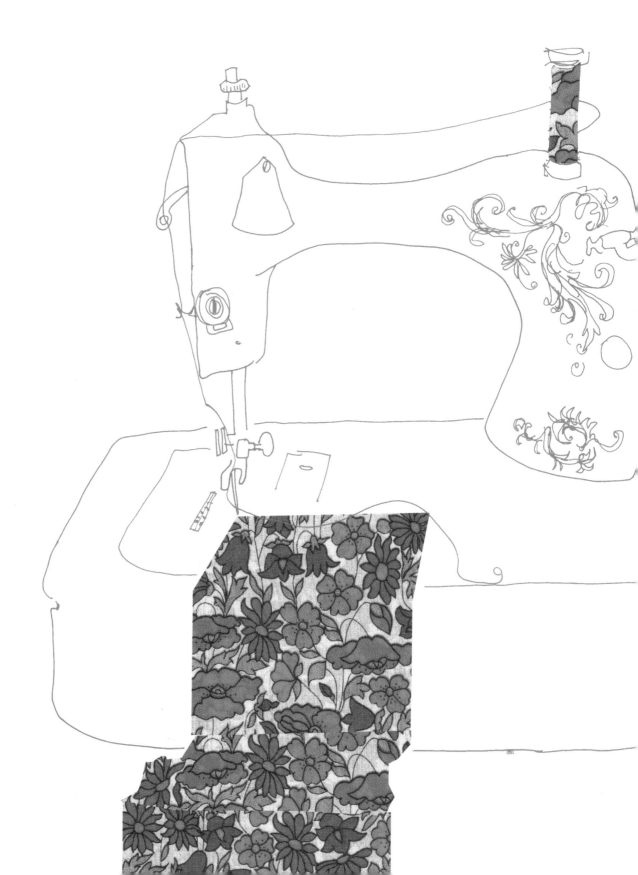

ALICE CHADWICK
& LEANNE FINN-DAVIS

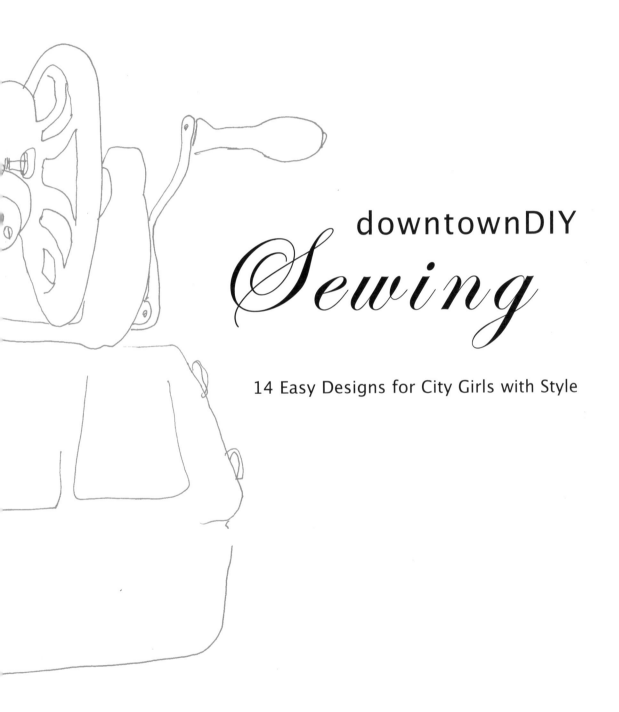

downtownDIY
Sewing

14 Easy Designs for City Girls with Style

Watson–Guptill Publications / New York

downtownDIY

Sewing

Contents

20: tote

22: mp3 player cover

24: off-the-
shoulder top

28: pencil skirt

32: lazy morning
PJ bottoms

36: necklace

38: tunic dress

42: summer shirt

46: t-shirt minidress

49: circle skirt

52: headband

54: circular bag

58: bows

60: puppy dog

4

Tools

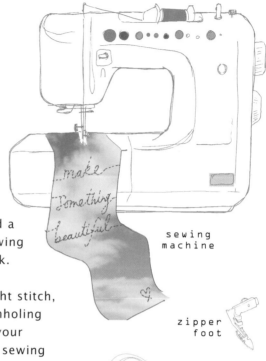

sewing
machine

You can get started with just a needle and thread and a pair of scissors – but a few basic items will make sewing easier and give a more professional look to your work.

A sewing machine offering basic features – a straight stitch, a zigzag stitch, adjustable stitch length, and a buttonholing function – is sufficient for most projects. Make sure your machine has a **zipper foot** for inserting zippers and sewing on piping.

zipper
foot

Keep a selection of machine needles on hand in case one breaks or becomes blunt (a blunt needle will snag fabric and skip stitches). You will need to match the size and type of needle to the weight of fabric you are using. The 2 most useful types of sewing machine needles are:
universal needle – a sharp-pointed needle used for most weights of woven fabrics.
ballpoint needle – a needle with a rounded point used for stretch knit fabrics.
Choose the correct needle size from the chart below.

scissors

Needle Size
for machines

NEEDLE SIZE (US/EURO)	FABRIC WEIGHT
8/60	fine & sheer
10/70	medium
12/80	medium
14/90	heavy (e.g., denim)
16/100	heavy (e.g., denim)
18/110	very heavy
19/120	very heavy

pinking shears

trimmer

seam ripper

styling design
ruler

tape measure

Measuring tools

tape measure

styling design ruler – for drafting patterns, drawing angles,
and measuring.

Marking tools

**dressmaker's marking pencil with brush eraser, tailor's chalk,
or water soluble marking pencil** – to transfer markings from the
pattern to the fabric. Keep your markers sharp. Use your scissor
blade to sharpen chalk.

Cutting tools

scissors or dressmaker's shears – a sharp pair of scissors or
dressmaker's shears at least 8 in. (20 cm) long for cutting fabric.
Use a different pair for cutting paper.

pinking shears – prevent fabric from fraying, create a decorative
zigzag edge, and are great for finishing seams.

trimmer – 4–6 in. (10–15 cm) long for snipping threads and notches,
and for clipping seam allowances.

seam ripper – for unpicking unwanted stitches.

Other tools

straight pins – for holding fabric together and position marking.

needles – an assorted package of sharps (medium-length needles
with round eyes) will give you a choice of size and provide
all-purpose needles for hand sewing.

safety pins – for threading elastic and pulling it
through casing.

pattern paper – for creating pattern pieces.

iron & ironing board – for pressing
seams and pattern pieces, and ironing
the assembled garment.

dressmaker's
marking pencil
with brush eraser

water soluble
marking pencil

tailor's
chalk

straight pins

needles

safety pins

pattern
paper

iron &   ironing board

Fabrics & threads

Fabric Your choice of fabric will depend on your desired finished look. It'll determine how you'll wear and wash your garment, how it will feel, and how long it will last. Keep these things in mind when you visit the fabric store or search the Internet. How about using a vintage fabric or recycling fabric from an old garment? There are 2 main types of fabric: **woven fabrics** *(01a)* have threads that cross at right angles, e.g., denim and flannel. **stretch knit fabrics** *(01b)* have threads that all run in one direction, e.g., jersey and Lycra.

Thread *(02)* For sewing seams, match thread color to fabric. For decorative topstitching, choose a thicker thread. The lower the number on the spool, the thicker the thread. How about using a contrasting color or picking up a color in the pattern detail?

Lining *(03)* is a separate layer of fabric that adds body and durability. It gives a beautiful inside finish, lets you slip the garment on and off easily, and protects your skin from scratchy fabrics such as wool.

Interfacing *(04)* is an extra layer of fabric that gives strength to areas taking more wear or needing a crisper form, such as shirt collars. Choose interfacing that's compatible with the weight, color, and stretch of your fabric. **Fusible** (iron-on) interfacing is easier to use, but sew-in is also available.

Notions

Zippers *(05a)* Choose a color that matches your fabric or makes a contrast into a feature.
Buttons *(05b)* can be matched, oversized, or mixed-and-matched.
Cording *(05c)* is used in a seamline to create a crisp decorative finish.
Elastic *(05d)* is used for easy on/off waistbands.
Sew-on snaps *(05e)* are simple press-together fasteners.
Bias tape *(05f)* is a strip of fabric used to make edges look neater. Cut on the bias, the fabric tape can stretch to fit around corners. Buy it ready made or make your own.

05c cording

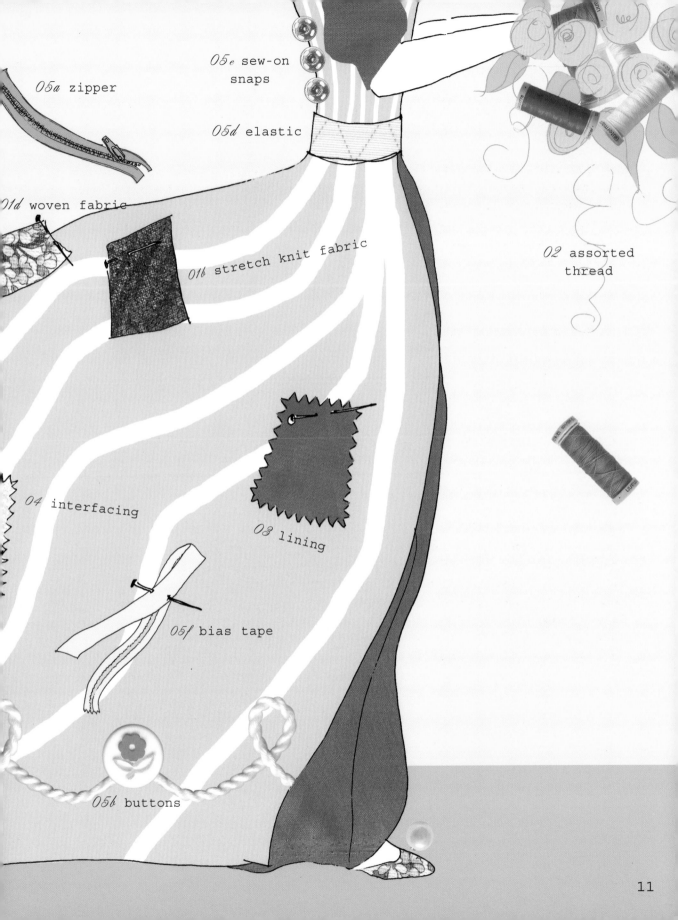

05a zipper

05e sew-on snaps

05d elastic

01d woven fabric

01b stretch knit fabric

02 assorted thread

04 interfacing

03 lining

05f bias tape

05b buttons

Using the patterns

The projects in this book have three different kinds of patterns. For the very simplest projects, you'll be asked to draw your own patterns on pattern paper, using specific dimensions. Slightly more involved projects include small-scale patterns for you to enlarge on a photocopier. And a last group has actual, full-scale patterns included in the book for you to cut out and use. Here's how to use each kind.

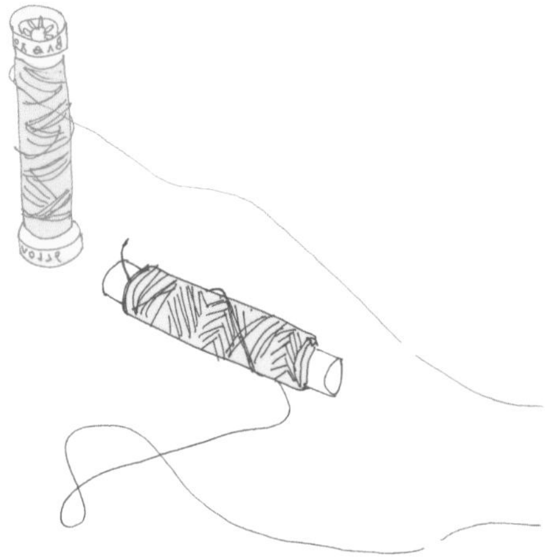

Preparing patterns

drawing your own patterns – Using a styling design ruler for right angles and a compass for circles, draw the pattern pieces, using the dimensions given in the written-out pattern, onto pattern paper. Mark the notches and grainline as instructed. Label each pattern piece by name as indicated by the capital letters, and include the number of each piece to cut.

photocopying patterns to scale – Look at the scaled pattern pieces. Scale up as indicated and copy the pattern pieces onto pattern paper.

using provided paper patterns – Determine your pattern size and cut out all of the pattern pieces for your chosen garment on the corresponding-sized cutting lines.

★★★ All patterns in this book have ⅜ in. (1 cm) seam allowance included. ★★★

Sizing

To determine the correct pattern size, compare your body measurements to the sizing chart below. Measure your bust and hips at the fullest part, your waist at the smallest. If you're between sizes, go for the bigger size; you can take it in later if necessary. You may be a different size for tops (bust measurement) than you are for skirts and pants (waist and hip measurements).

Sizing Chart

	US inch	UK (EURO) cm	US inch	UK (EURO) cm	US inch	UK (EURO) cm	US inch	UK (EURO) cm
PATTERN SIZE	6	8 (34)	8	10 (36)	10	12 (38)	12	14 (40)
waist	25	63	26½	67	28	71	29½	75
bust	32½	82	34	86	35½	90	37	94
hips	34½	87	36	91	37½	95	39	99

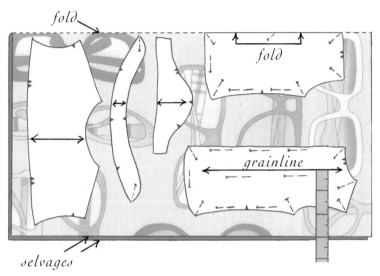

fold

fold

grainline

selvages

laying the pattern on the fabric

Pattern markings

Pattern markings (see chart on page 19) are used on paper patterns to provide information on:

laying & cutting fabric

Before you start, see if your fabric has a nap. **Nap** refers to a fabric with a direction: either a pile, such as velvet, or a patterned design that has one way up. All pattern pieces cut on a fabric with a nap should be laid with the tops going in the same direction (see diagram above).

1 Fold fabric lengthwise, with right sides together, selvage (lengthwise fabric edge) to selvage.

2 Lay pattern pieces that need to go on the fold. Edge of pattern piece goes on fold of fabric. Pin in place. Lay other pieces on fabric to complete pattern layout. Do not place edges of pattern pieces on selvage.

3 Grainlines should be parallel to selvage. Pin one end of grainline, measure distance of grainline to selvage or fold, move other end of grainline until it measures the same distance, and pin.

4 Pin around rest of pattern, corners first.

5 Cut fabric around pattern pieces, with fabric flat on the table. Keep pattern to the left (to right if left-handed) of scissors as you cut, using the whole blade.

marking

1 Snip notches and end-of-fold lines with tip of scissors.

2 Transfer positioning marks, e.g., position of pocket, onto fabric by pinning through pattern and 2 layers of fabric, marking position point on wrong side of both layers.

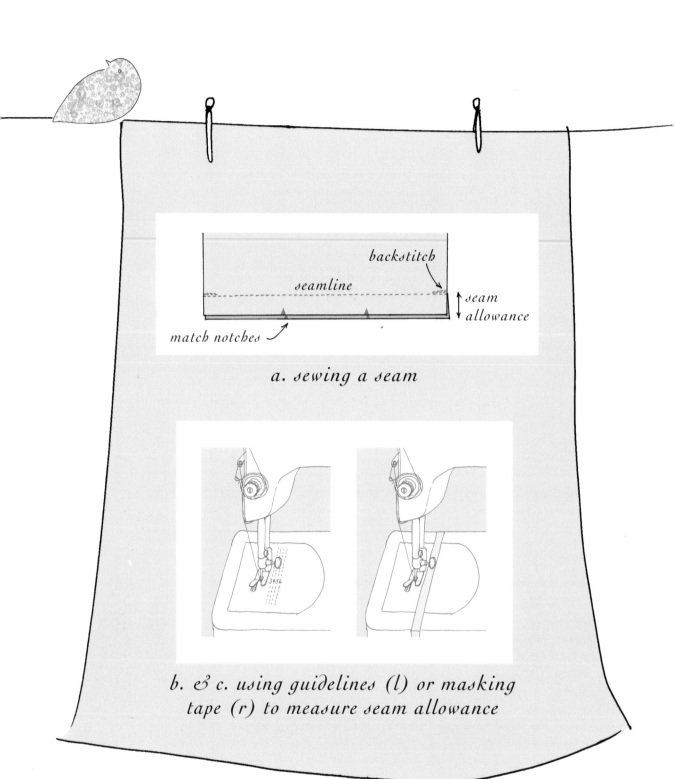

backstitch

seamline

match notches

seam allowance

a. sewing a seam

b. & c. using guidelines (l) or masking
tape (r) to measure seam allowance

Sewing techniques

Before starting, make sure you know your sewing machine well. Read the manufacturer's handbook thoroughly and do LOTS of practicing.

Stitches

Straight stitch is used for seams, darts, and tucks. Stitch length depends on weight of fabric, with finer fabric needing smaller stitches, heavier fabric larger stitches.

Backstitch is used to anchor a seam and reinforce the permanent stitches at the beginning and end of every line of sewing. Press the reverse stitch button on your machine to sew backward and forward in the same place (illus. a).

Basting stitch is temporary stitching used to secure fabric in place before using a permanent straight stitch. Use the longest stitch length on your machine and don't backstitch.

Seams

Seams are used to join fabric. There are different ways of seaming fabric together, depending on the type of fabric, type of garment, or look that you want.

A **plain seam** is the most common:

1 Place right side of fabric pieces together, with the edges to be joined and any notches matching (illus. a).

2 Pin seams to secure.

3 Use seam guidelines (illus. b) – or masking tape stuck parallel ⅜ in. (1 cm) from the needle on your machine (illus. c) – to get an accurate, even seam allowance, starting and finishing with ¼ in. (5 mm) of backstitch. Snip threads as you finish each seam.

Seam allowance (SA) is the distance between seamline and edge of fabric (illus. a). All seam allowances are ⅜ in. (1 cm) on pattern pieces in this book unless otherwise stated.

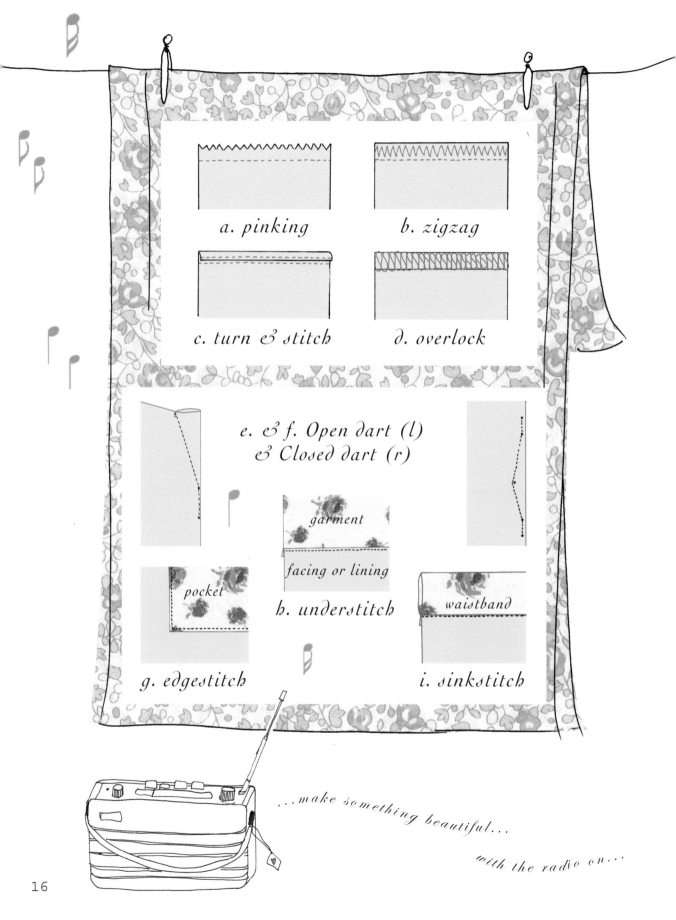

a. pinking

b. zigzag

c. turn & stitch

d. overlock

e. & f. Open dart (l)
& Closed dart (r)

garment

facing or lining

h. understitch

pocket

g. edgestitch

waistband

i. sinkstitch

...make something beautiful...

with the radio on...

Seam finishing

Seam finishing neatens raw edges of fabric after sewing a seam and stops fabric from fraying. Choose one of the following methods:

pinking Trim with pinking shears for a quick, easy finish (illus. a).

zigzag Do a zigzag stitch along the edge (illus. b).

turn & stitch Turn edge ⅛ in. (3 mm) under to wrong side, stitch close to edge (illus. c).

overlock Used in industrial clothing production. Use if you own an overlocking machine (illus d).

press Lay garment wrong side up on an ironing board. Use a steam iron to press SA down as you go, after each stage of sewing.

More stitching

Darts give contour to a garment.

⁄ Open (straight tapered) darts come from the edge of the fabric and are sewn into a seam, e.g., on skirts or pants at the waist, or on a top for the bust. Match notches at edge of fabric, with fabric folding to point of dart. Stitch from top of dart down to first-position mark, stopping one stitch before you get to the fold, then stitch along, close to fold edge, until point of dart (illus. e).

Vertical darts, press on wrong side toward side seams. Horizontal darts, press on wrong side downward.

2 Closed (also called double-ended or fisheye) darts form contour for bust, waist, and hips in one dart.

Fold from top-dart point to bottom-dart point with waist points matching. Secure with straight pins. Stitch from top, along the fold edge to 2nd-position mark, out to waist and down, running along the edge to finish (illus. f).

Tucks give fullness to a garment. Fold tucks, matching notches, making sure pleat is absolutely straight. Baste in place across tuck, inside of seamline (see illus. a; page 31).

Edgestitch is used to stitch close along a folded or seamed edge (illus. g).

Understitch is used to prevent a facing or lining from showing on the outside of a garment. With all SA pushed away from the garment, stitch on right side of facing or lining, close to seam edge (illus. h).

Sinkstitch is a hidden line of stitches used to complete attachment of waistbands, collars, cuffs, and binding. Stitch into ridge of seam on right side of garment to catch and hold down SA on wrong side (illus. i).

gathering Pulls fabric together along a stitchline to create fullness. Sew 2 rows of long basting stitches on either side of SA. Tug bobbin threads (threads on wrong side of fabric) to gather to required measurement. Knot threads at each end to hold gathering in place (illus. a). Attach fabric to garment and unpick basting stitch.

slipstitch is an invisible hand-sewn stitch for finishing.
1 Uneven slipstitch is used to finish hems or facings.
a Pick up a small, inconspicuous thread of the garment fabric with the needle, next to where the hem is sitting.
b Make another stitch by placing the point of the needle into the fold of the hem's turned-over raw edge and running the needle along the inside of the fold for ⅜ in. (1 cm).
c Repeat until finished (illus. b).
2 Even slipstitch is used to join edges of an opening. Place the point of the needle into the folded edge of one side of the opening and run the needle along the inside of the fold for ⅜ in. (1 cm). Repeat on other side of the opening, starting on the opposite side of where you finished the last stitch (illus. c).

Fusing interfacing
Use a steam iron to attach fusable interfacing. Adhesive side (can feel dots of glue on one side) sticks to wrong side of fabric.

Abbreviations used in book

WS	wrong side of fabric
RS	right side of fabric
SA	seam allowance
CB	center back
CF	center front
bk	back
frt	front
SNP	shoulder neck point

a. gathering

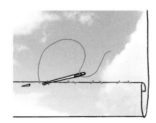

b. uneven slipstich

c. even slipstitch

Pattern Markings

a.

f. — — — — — —

b. ✂

g. ⊢—⊠

c.

h. ∧∧∧∧∧∧∧∧∧

d.

i. └┘

e.

j. ○

a. CUTTING LINE – cut on line indicating your size.

b. CUTTING LINE FOR LINING – after cutting fabric, use pattern to cut lining on this line.

c. ON THE FOLD – lay pattern edge on fold of fabric.

d. GRAINLINE – runs parallel to selvage.

e. NOTCH – match notches on corresponding seams. Snip into fabric edge ¼ in. (5 mm) to mark. 2 notches indicate a piece that is at the back of the garment.

f. SEAMLINE – sew garment pieces together along this line.

g. BUTTONHOLE POSITION and BUTTON – buttonholes are marked as horizontal or vertical I-bars. Buttons are marked with an X.

h. ZIPPER POSITION

i. GATHERING – gather stitches between notches on pattern to indicated finished measurement.

j. POSITIONING MARK – mark on fabric to indicate details, e.g., position of pocket.

01 tote

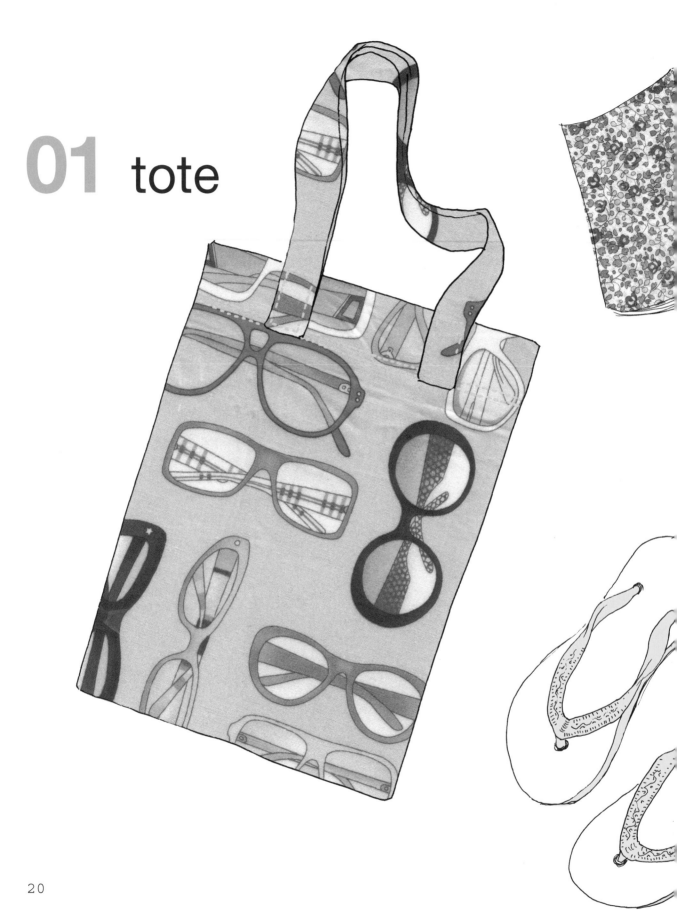

what you need:

materials:
29 in. (74 cm) medium-/heavy-weight fabric

finished size:
11 x 12½ in. (27.5 x 31.5 cm)*
*excluding handles

A simple tote, with 2 shoulder straps and enough space for a book, sunglasses, and a bikini. Can be cut and sewn together in an hour (or less) – and then off to the beach!

To cut out

BAG: 29 x 12 in. (74 x 30 cm) – CUT 1
HANDLE: 21 x 2¾ in. (53 x 7 cm) – CUT 2

To make the tote

To make the bag

1 Fold BAG across in half, RS together.
2 Sew side seams.
3 Fold top edge under ⅜ in. (1 cm) toward the inside. Press.
4 Fold top edge under again 1½ in. (4 cm). Press.
5 From inside, sew ¼ in. (5 mm) from turned-over edge.
6 Turn the bag RS out.

To make the handles

1 Fold each HANDLE in half lengthwise, RS together, and sew along seamline.
2 Turn the handle RS out. Press flat with seam on edge of handle.
3 Lay ends of handles toward top of bag, ⅝ in. (1.5 cm) above top stitchline and 2¾ in. (7 cm) from side seams.
4 From outside, sew parallel ⅛ in. (3 mm) below existing stitchline, stitching over the 2 ends of each handle as you go (illus. a).
5 Push handles upward.
6 Sew a rectangle through base of each handle to secure handle in place (illus. b).

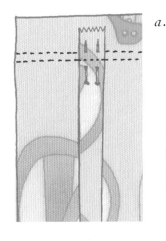

a.

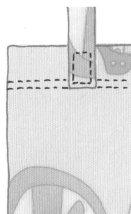

b

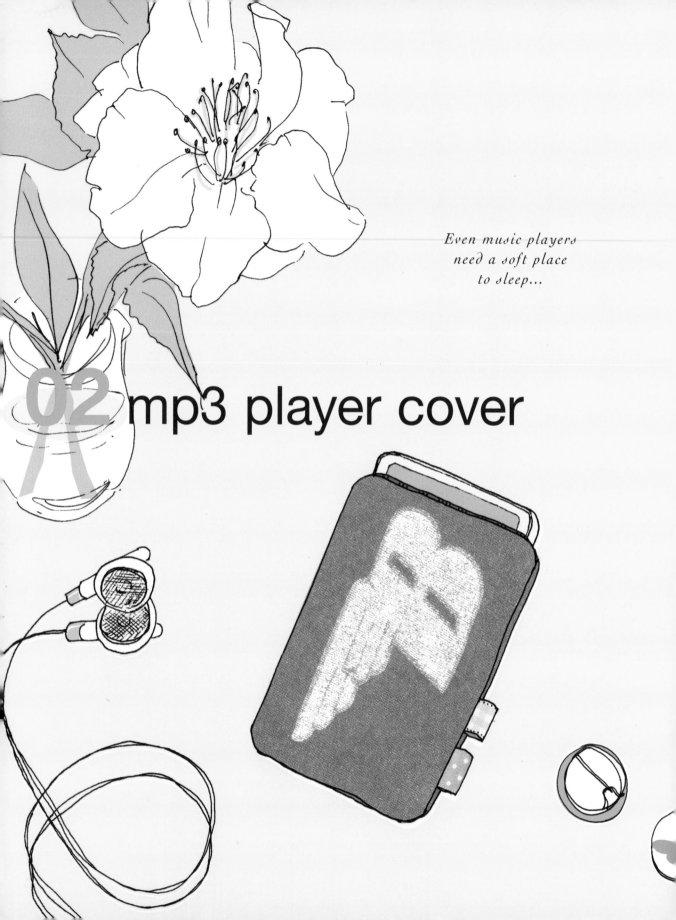

*Even music players
need a soft place
to sleep...*

02 mp3 player cover

$\mathscr{W}$hat can you do when your favorite rock T-shirt falls apart? Cut it up and make this mp3 cover! This is sewing at its simplest – a little pocket, lined to give a snug fit and finished with a dash of colored ribbon.

what you need:

materials:
fabric for cover & contrasting fabric for lining*
*enough to cover your mp3 player
2 in. (5 cm) of ribbon

$\mathscr{T}$o cut out

Measure your mp3 player, making note of: width of 1 side plus width of the front, and length of the front plus width of the base. Add ¾ in. (2 cm) to each measurement. Cut a rectangle with these dimensions from 2 layers of outer fabric and 2 layers of lining fabric.

5 Turn RS out.
6 Turn raw edges of lining under ¼ in. (5 mm) and edgestitch them together across width (illus. c).
7 Push lining into outer pocket. Press top edge.

$\mathscr{T}$o make the cover

1 Fold ribbon in half and position it on RS of 1 outer fabric piece, with cut edges facing out, 1½ in. (4 cm) up from bottom right-hand corner. Baste inside of seamline to secure in place (illus. a).
2 Sew outer fabric piece with ribbon to 1 lining piece, RS together, along end width where ribbon is attached. Sew other outer and lining pieces together along seamlines. Open seams and press.
3 Lay 2 strips RS together, outer layers on top of each other and lining layers on top of each other.
4 Starting with lining fabric, sew along one length at seamline, across width of outer fabric, and along other side. Cut corners at an angle (illus. b).

a.

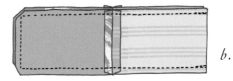

b.

c.

how about...making the cover in plain fabric and adding a pin or two?

03 off-the-shoulder top

*J*ust one of the things you have to have – a T-shirt in striped jersey with batwing (or dolman) sleeves and a wide neck. For the girl about the beach, festival, bagel shop...

what you need:

tools:
styling design ruler

materials:
2¼ yd. (2 m) of 35/45 in. (90/115 cm) wide stretch knit fabric
or ⅓ yd. (120 cm) of 60 in. (150 cm) wide stretch knit fabric
6 in. (15 cm) interfacing
pattern paper

To cut out

BODY – CUT 2

1 Draw a rectangle 44 x 22 in. (112 x 56 cm).
2 Divide the rectangle in half so you have 2 x 22 in. (56 cm) squares.
3 Work inside the right-hand square.
4 Divide each side of the square in half and join the points to divide the square into 4. Mark the center where the lines cross with a B (illus. a; page 27).
5 From bottom left-hand corner, for **size 6–8**, mark point A on the line, 9½ in. (24 cm) across; for **size 10–12**, 10 in. (25 cm) across.
6 From top right-hand corner, mark point C on the line 5¾ in. (14.5 cm) down.
7 Join A to B to C with a smooth curve.
8 From top left-hand corner, mark a point on the line 5⅜ in. (13.5 cm) across, and then mark a point 3 in. (7.5 cm) down from the corner.
9 Join these points with a curve to create the neckline.
10 The left edge of the square is the CF line. Fold the pattern paper along this line and cut around the garment shape you have drafted.
11 Mark the grainline across the garment perpendicular to the CF line.
12 Label this pattern piece: BODY – CUT 2

NECK FACING – CUT 2 + CUT 2 INTERFACING

On BODY, draw a curve 3¼ in. (8 cm) from neckline. Trace around shape created between curve and neckline, and shoulder lines.

CUFF – CUT 2

Draw a rectangle 6¼ x 10⅝ in. (16 x 27 cm). Mark notches at center of longest edge on both sides.

BELLYBAND – CUT 1

Draw a rectangle:
size 6–8: 8 x 36 in. (20 x 91 cm);
size 10–12: 8 x 37⅜ in. (20 x 95 cm).
Mark notches at center of longest edge on both sides.

Cut pattern pieces on single layer of fabric.

Fuse interfacing to NECK FACING.

To assemble the top

To assemble the body

Sew 2 BODY pieces together, along shoulder seamline and along underarm seamline.

To attach the bellyband

1 Join ends of the BELLYBAND.
2 Fold bellyband in half lengthwise, WS together, and baste edges together inside of seamline.
3 Matching bellyband seam and notch to side seams of body, sew BELLYBAND to bottom edge of BODY.

To attach the cuffs

1 Join ends of each CUFF.
2 Fold cuff in half lengthwise, WS together, and baste edges together inside of seamline.
3 Matching cuff seam to underarm seam on body and cuff notch to overarm seam on body, sew CUFF to edge of sleeve on BODY.

To prepare & attach the neck facing

1 Join shoulder seams of NECK FACING.
2 Trim outer edge of facing.
3 Sew neck edge of FACING to neck edge of BODY, matching shoulder seams.
4 Trim SA to ¼ in. (5 mm).
5 Understitch around facing neck edge.

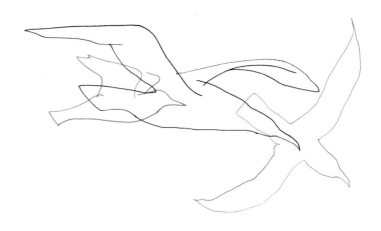

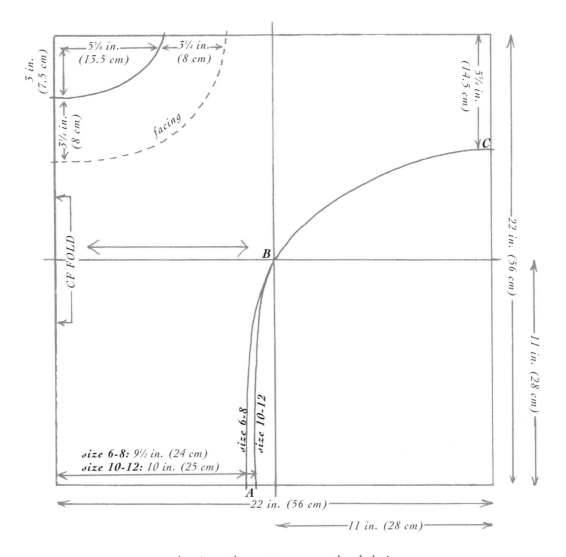

5 in.
(7.5 cm)

5⁵⁄₈ in.
(13.5 cm)

3¼ in.
(8 cm)

3¼ in.
(8 cm)

facing

5¾ in.
(14.5 cm)

C

22 in. (56 cm)

11 in. (28 cm)

CF FOLD

B

size 6-8

size 10-12

size 6-8: 9½ in. (24 cm)
size 10-12: 10 in. (25 cm)

A

22 in. (56 cm)

11 in. (28 cm)

a. laying the pattern on the fabric

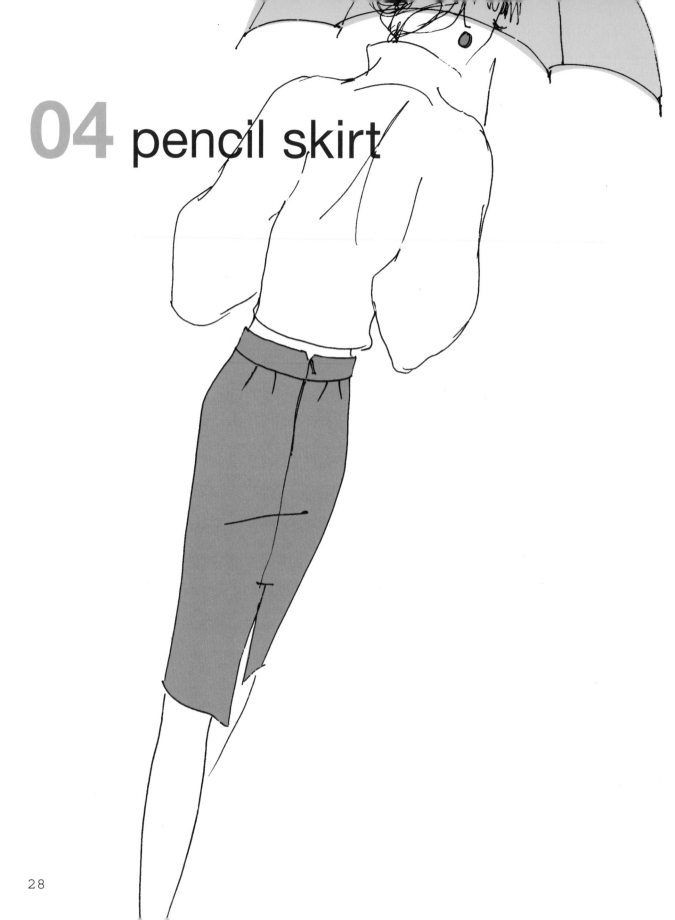

04 pencil skirt

This straight skirt is both smart and sexy. Falling to just below the knee, it has a back slit and darts to give a tailored profile. And it's lined for that swish-swish feeling. Knock 'em dead!

To cut out

Use pattern on pattern sheets provided.
Cut out all PENCIL SKIRT pattern pieces along cutting line of your size.
To make FRT and BK LINING patterns, trace FRT and BK SKIRT patterns onto pattern paper, cutting away excess hem and around slit on "Cut for Lining" line as indicated on FRT and BK SKIRT patterns.
Cut indicated number of pattern pieces on folded double layer of fabric.

Fuse interfacing onto WAISTBAND.

To make the skirt

To sew the tucks & darts
1 Fold tucks on FRT SKIRT with notch nearest CF on top of notch nearest side seam and matching positioning marks. Baste in place across tuck, inside of seamline (illus. a; page 31).
2 Sew tapered darts on BK SKIRT.

To prepare the CB seam
Sew along CB seamline from notch at bottom of zipper opening down to position mark at top of CB slit.

what you need:

tools:
zipper foot
hand-sewing needle

materials:
⅞ yd. (80 cm) of 45/56 in. (115/150 cm) wide medium-/heavy-weight woven fabric
¾ yd. (65 cm) light-weight lining
6 in. (15 cm) interfacing
6 in. (15 cm) zipper
hook & bar
pattern paper

To insert the zipper
1 Baste together zipper opening.
2 Open zipper and pin it, correct side down, onto WS of skirt, with edge of zipper teeth along basted seamline (illus. b; page 31).
3 Using zipper foot and starting from top edge, stitch ⅜ in. (1 cm) away from zipper teeth, down to zipper position notch. Stop with needle down. Lift zipper foot and close zipper. Pivot fabric around to stitch across end of zipper. Stop with needle down again. Lift zipper foot, pivot fabric around to sew other side of zipper, ⅜ in. (1 cm) from zipper teeth, up to top edge of skirt.
4 Remove basting stitches and press (illus. c; page 31).
5 Join FRT to BK SKIRT pieces at side seams.

To make & attach the lining

1 Sew frt tucks as for skirt on FRT LINING. Sew bk tapered darts as for skirt on BK LINING.

2 Join CB seam.

3 Finish zipper opening by turning raw edge under ¼ in. (5 mm), then under again ⅜ in. (1 cm) and sewing down. Finish slit opening in same way.

4 Join side seams.

5 Finish hem by turning raw edge under and sewing (step 3).

6 Attach lining to skirt, placing WS together and matching seams. Baste top waist edges inside of seamline.

To prepare the waistband

1 Fold WAISTBAND in half lengthwise, RS together.

2 Sew seams together at one end.

3 Sew extension end, from folded edge down, then across to notch. Cut corners at an angle and trim SA to ¼ in. (5 mm) (illus. d).

4 Turn waistband RS out. Press.

To attach the waistband

1 Open the zipper.

2 With extension end of waistband on right side of zipper and straight seamed end of waistband lined up exactly with left edge of zipper, pin RS of one layer of waistband to the RS top edge of the skirt.

3 Sew waistband to skirt (illus. e).

4 Turning SA of other edge of waistband under, pin perpendicularly along folded edge just over last stitchline.

5 From outside of skirt, sinkstitch through waistband seam, sewing down waistband on inside of skirt.

To finish the hem & back slit

1 To join hem to slit facing, bring points X (illus. f) RS together, sewing diagonal seam from corner to edges (illus. g).

2 Trim SA at corner. Press seam open and turn RS out.

3 Press fold of slit from hem corner to top of slit.

4 Press hem up along hem fold line. Sew an uneven slipstitch to finish hem.

5 Reinforce slit opening by sewing 2 rows of stitching on top of each other along bottom of CB seamline, ⅜ in. (1 cm) in length, at place indicated by positioning mark on pattern (illus. h).

To attach hook & bar

1 Position hook on inside of left-hand side of waistband, ¼ in. (5 mm) from end, in the center. Hand-stitch hook onto fabric using doubled-over and knotted thread, making sure that stitches don't come through to RS of waistband.

2 Close zipper and mark where hook meets other side of waistband for bar position. Hand-stitch bar in place (illus. i).

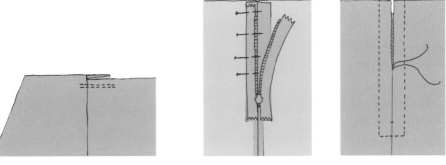

a. sewing the tuck

b. & c. inserting the zipper

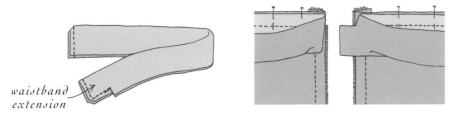

waistband
extension

d. & e. preparing (l) & attaching (r) the waistband

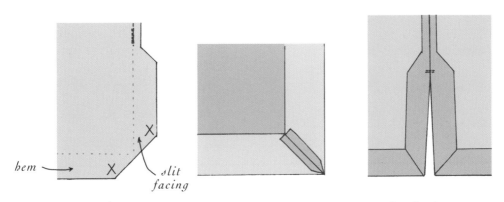

hem

slit
facing

f., g., & h. finishing the hem (l & center) & back slit (r)

i. attaching the hook & bar

05 lazy morning pj bottoms

what you need:

tools:
styling design ruler
safety pin

materials:
1⅛ yd. (110 cm) of 60 in. (150 cm) wide
light-/medium-weight woven cotton
or 2¼ yd. (2 m) of 45 in. (115 cm) wide
light-/medium-weight woven cotton
10 in. (25 cm) contrasting light-/
medium-weight woven cotton
31½ in. (80 cm) of ¾ in. (2 cm) wide
elastic
pattern paper

It's been quite a night...and now morning is here. What do you wear when you only half want to get up? Throw these pj bottoms on with a T-shirt and enjoy a gentle start to the day. Who says you have to get up and get dressed?

To cut out

Enlarge small-scale patterns (see page 35) to 590%.
Cut out all PAJAMA BOTTOM pattern pieces along cutting line of your size.
Also cut the following:
WAISTBAND: 2½ in. (6.5 cm) x waistband measurement – CUT 1
HEM BAND: 1⅜ in. (3.5 cm) x hem band measurement – CUT 2

Sizing Chart

	US inch	UK (EURO) cm	US inch	UK (EURO) cm	US inch	UK (EURO) cm	US inch	UK (EURO) cm
PATTERN SIZE	6	8 (34)	8	10 (36)	10	12 (38)	12	14 (40)
waistband	36¼	92	37¾	96	39⅜	100	41	104
hem band	23⅛	59.5	24¼	61.5	25	63.5	25¾	65.5
cut elastic	29⅛	74	30¾	78	32¼	82	33⅞	86

To make the pj bottoms

To make & attach the pocket

1 With POCKET pieces RS together, sew along seamline, starting at bottom point of heart shape and ending about 2 in. (5 cm) before you are back at the bottom point of heart.

2 Trim SA to ¼ in. (5 mm), and clip around curves and into top point, up to but not through stitching (illus. a).

3 Turn RS out.

4 Press flat, turning under SA of opening.

5 Edgestitch around heart.

6 Mark pocket notches with straight pins.

7 Position pocket notches onto pocket positioning marks on right FRT PAJAMA leg. Pin flat onto leg.

8 Attach pocket by edgestitching, on top of existing stitchline, between pocket positioning marks, on the lower half of heart shape.

9 Reinforce pocket opening by backstitching a row of 2 or 3 stitches several times at top of edgestitching (illus. b).

To attach the hem bands

1 Join FRT and BK PAJAMA side seams.

2 Sew HEM BAND to bottom edge of pajama leg, with RS hem band to WS pajama leg (illus. c).

3 Fold hem band up onto RS pajama leg, with seam at bottom edge of pajama leg. Press. Turn top hem band SA under. Press.

4 Working from RS pajama leg, edgestitch top of hem band to attach (illus. d).

5 Repeat for other pajama leg.

To make the pajama legs

1 Join frt to bk inside leg seams.

2 Turn one leg RS out and the other leg WS out.

3 Put RS-out leg inside WS-out leg, matching inside leg seams and notches along crotch seam. Sew crotch seam. Clip around curves up to but not through stitching (illus. e).

To make the elasticized waist

1 Sew ends of WAISTBAND together along seamline. This seam is placed at CB.

2 With RS waistband to RS pajama, sew top edge along seamline.

3 Turn other waistband SA under. Press.

4 Fold waistband over WS of top pajama edge with folded SA edge just covering pajama stitchline. Pin vertically (illus. f).

5 From RS at CB, edgestitch waistband down, leaving 1¼ in. (3 cm) unstitched opening at CB.

6 Cut elastic to correct length (see chart on page 33). Attach safety pin to one end of elastic.

7 Securing one end of elastic at CB with a straight pin, thread elastic through waistband casing (illus. g).

8 Pull ends of elastic through opening. Lay one end on top of the other end and stitch a square to secure (illus. h).

9 Sew down through CB waistband seam to secure elastic in place and finish opening with edgestitch from RS (illus. h).

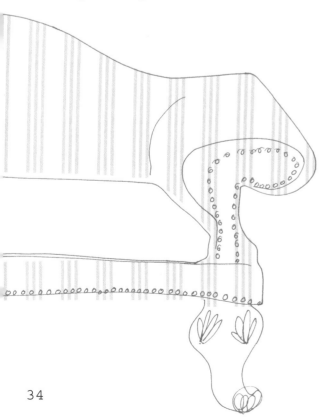

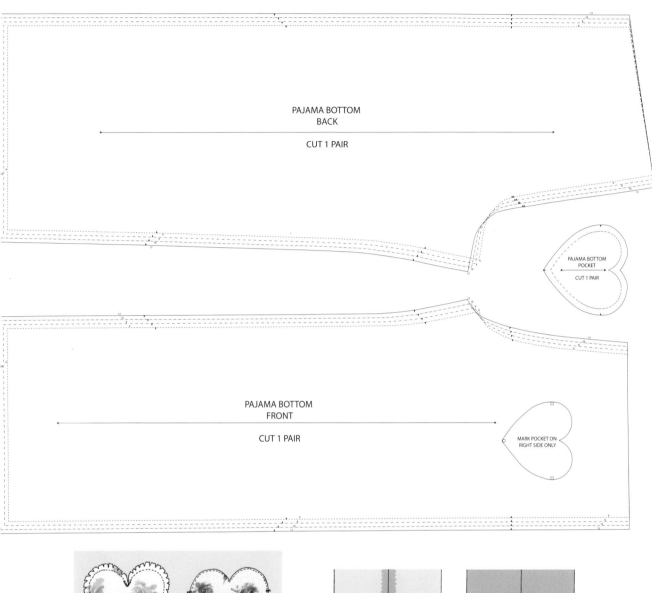

PAJAMA BOTTOM
BACK

CUT 1 PAIR

PAJAMA BOTTOM
POCKET

CUT 1 PAIR

PAJAMA BOTTOM
FRONT

CUT 1 PAIR

MARK POCKET ON
RIGHT SIDE ONLY

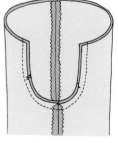

*a. & b. making (l) &
attaching (r) the pocket*

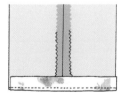

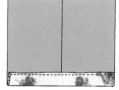

c. & d. attaching the hem band

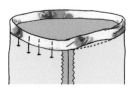

e. making the legs

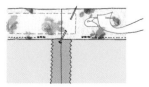
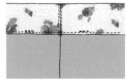

f., g., & h. making the elasticized waist

06 necklace

what you need:

tools:
large safety pin

materials:
4 x 53 in. (10 x 135 cm) strip of fabric
6 x 1¼ in. (3 cm)-diameter beads

*W*hen you need a necklace to turn a few heads, this is the one to make. Using only a handful of beads, a tube of fabric, and some well-tied knots, this choker will transform a vest and jeans into an outfit fit for a party. Go, Cinderella!

To make the necklace

1 Make a tube by folding fabric lengthwise, RS together, and sewing along seamline.
2 Attach a large safety pin to one end of the tube. Push it through the tube to turn tube RS out.
3 Tie first knot about 11½ in. (30 cm) from one end.
4 Push 1 bead into the tube from the unknotted end until it meets the knot snuggly.
5 Tie another knot close to the bead.

6 Repeat steps 4 and 5 for all the beads.
7 Make sure that the tube ends are of equal length from the end knots. Trim ends diagonally.
8 Turn in the raw ends ¼ in. (5 mm).
9 Sew even slipstitches to close the ends.

07 tunic dress

what you need:

materials:
1⅞ yd. (170 cm) of 45 in. (115 cm) wide
or 1¼ yd. (110 cm) of 60 in. (150 cm) wide
medium-weight fabric
1¼ yd. (110 cm) of lining
1 yd. (1 m) bias tape
6 in. (15 cm) interfacing
pattern paper

𝒯his is one of those magical garments – a dress that you will always feel fantastic in. Wear it with jeans, leggings, striped tights – it has a great shape, cute lined pockets, and an elegant funnel neck. Do you look good? Of course you do!

To cut out

Use pattern on pattern sheets provided.
Cut out all TUNIC DRESS pattern pieces along cutting line of your size.
Make a collar interfacing pattern by folding COLLAR pattern in half lengthwise.
Fold collar piece in half lengthwise and fuse interfacing to one half of collar.

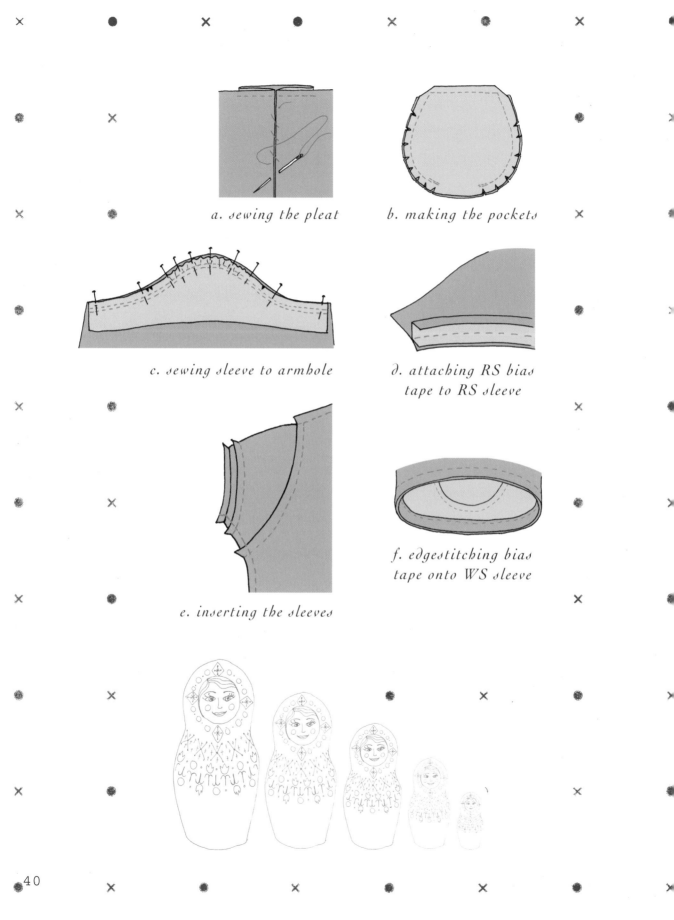

a. sewing the pleat

b. making the pockets

c. sewing sleeve to armhole

d. attaching RS bias tape to RS sleeve

e. inserting the sleeves

f. edgestitching bias tape onto WS sleeve

To make the tunic dress

To sew the darts & pleat

1 Sew closed darts on the BK DRESS.
2 Join CB seam.
3 Sew bust darts on FRT DRESS, joining edges of dart cut into pattern piece under armhole and extending dart to positioning mark indicated for size.
4 Fold CF pleat with positioning marks meeting, to match at CF (illus. a; page 40).
5 Baste along inside of seamline on neck edge to secure pleat in place.
6 Overstitch CF pleat fold together to secure in place, ending stitching at positioning mark indicated for size (illus. a; page 40).

To make & attach the pockets

1 Place RS lining over RS POCKET. Starting at bottom, sew together around outside edge, leaving 1½ in. (4 cm) unstitched opening to finish.
2 Trim SA to ¼ in. (5 mm), clip corners at an angle and around curves up to but not through stitching (illus. b).
3 Turn RS out.
4 Turn SA of opening under and press flat.
5 Position corners of pocket onto pocket positioning marks on FRT DRESS. Pin flat onto dress.
6 Edgestitch around pocket curve to attach.

To make & attach the collar

1 Join frt and bk shoulder seams.
2 Sew CB seams of COLLAR together to form a circle.
3 Fold collar in half lengthwise, WS together. Baste neck edges together inside seamline.
4 With dress WS out, position collar with collar CB seam matching dress CB seam and side of collar without interfacing to RS dress. Sew collar neck edge to dress neck edge.

To insert the sleeves

1 Matching notches, pin SLEEVE to armhole, distributing the extra fabric on the sleeve evenly.
2 Sew sleeve to armhole with ¼ in. (5 mm) SA. Sew again, using correct SA (illus. c).
3 Place RS bias tape along RS sleeve hem edge. Sew through bias tape at the fold to attach (illus. d).
4 Sew side seams together. Start by sewing bias tape, then sleeve hem edge, then underarm, and then down to hem (illus. e).
5 Turn bias tape to WS of sleeve, with existing bias tape stitchline at hem edge.
6 With other bias tape edge turned under, edgestitch bias tape onto WS sleeve (illus. f).

To finish the hem

1 Unpick CF pleat overstitching.
2 Turn hem edge under ⅜ in. (1 cm). Press. Turn under again 1¼ in. (3 cm). From WS of dress, edgestitch hem in place. Press, making sure CF pleat folds are pressed well at hem.

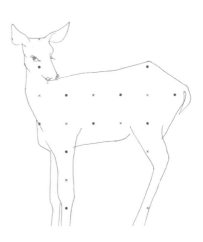

08 summer shirt

⊶⊷—— ⊶⊷——

what you need:

materials:
45 in. (115 cm) of 45/60 in. (115/150 cm)
wide light-/medium-weight woven fabric
8 in. (20 cm) interfacing
5 x ³⁄₈ in. (1 cm)-diameter buttons
16 in. (41 cm) of ³⁄₈ in. (1 cm) wide ribbon
cut into 2 x 8 in. (20.5 cm) pieces
pattern paper

*T*he sun is shining and the birds are singing...and this little fitted shirt is perfect for summer. With its cute gathered sleeves and ribbon detailing on the yoke, it's as pretty as a summer's day!

To cut out

Use pattern on pattern sheets provided. Cut out all SHIRT pattern pieces along cutting line of your size.

Fuse interfacing to FRT FACING and to 1 COLLAR piece.

To make the shirt

1 Gather FRT SHIRT between notches where indicated on pattern piece so that gathered fabric ends up measuring 2 in. (5 cm).
2 Sew SHIRT SIDE BK PANELS to SHIRT CENTER BK PANEL along seamlines.
3 Sew FRT FACINGS to CF edge of FRT SHIRT with RS together. Trim SA to ¼ in. (5 mm). Clip outer corner at an angle and clip into inner corner. Trim facing edge (illus. a; page 44). Turn RS out.
4 Understitch facing from hem to corner as far as possible. Press.

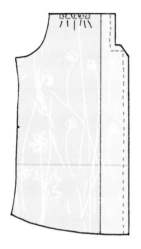

a. trimming facing edges

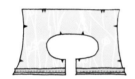

b. securing ribbon to yoke

c. attaching the yoke

d. preparing the collar

To prepare & attach the yoke

1 On 1 YOKE piece, place ribbon along the RS of the frt seamline, ⅛ in. (3 mm) from edge. Baste stitch inside of SA to secure ribbon (illus b).

2 Place 2 YOKE pieces one on top of the other with RS together, and sew CF seams together. Trim SA to ¼ in. (5 mm).

3 Sandwich FRT SHIRT pieces between 2 layers of yoke, the ribboned yoke seam facing the RS of the shirt. Make sure CF edge of frt shirt is right against CF seam of yoke. Sew yoke frt seams. Trim corner at CF seam (illus. c).

4 Pulling frt shirt pieces to one side through armhole openings, sandwich BK SHIRT between bk yoke pieces, matching notches to side panel seams. Sew back yoke seams. Turn yoke RS out.

To prepare the collar

1 With RS together, sew top curved edge of COLLAR (illus. d).

2 Trim SA to ¼ in. (5 mm) and clip around curves up to but not through stitching.

3 Turn collar RS out.

To attach the collar

1 With RS of shirt facing up, pin only the RS of interfaced layer of collar to neck edge of shirt. Make sure frt edge of collar and frt edge of shirt match exactly. Sew (illus. e).

2 Trim SA to ¼ in. (5 mm).

3 Press SA up toward collar and also press the ⅜ in. (1 cm) SA of the unsewn collar edge under.

4 Place unsewn collar SA just over neckline seam stitches. Pin perpendicular to seamline (illus. f).

5 Leaving pins in, edgestitch along collar neck seam from RS of garment through all layers of fabric to attach collar. Remove pins (illus. g).

To prepare & attach the sleeves

1 Gather SLEEVE hemline between notches where indicated on pattern piece so that gathered fabric ends up measuring 2¾ in. (7 cm).
2 Fold CUFF in half lengthwise, WS together.
3 Sew cuff onto sleeve along sleeve hemline (illus. h).
4 Press cuff down, SA up.
5 Gather sleeve cap between notches where indicated on pattern piece so that gathered fabric ends up measuring 2½ in. (6.5 cm) from center notch to frt sleeve notch and 2⅜ in. (6 cm) from center notch to bk sleeve notch.
6 Matching notches, pin sleeve to armhole. Sew along seamline.
7 Sew side seams, starting at cuff, along underarm and down sides of shirt.

To hem the shirt

1 Fold hemline under ¼ in. (5 mm). Press. Fold under again ⅜ in. (1 cm). Edgestitch from WS of shirt.

To make the buttonholes

1 Make buttonholes on right-hand side of shirt (see p. 51), as per marked lengths and positions.
2 Sew buttons onto RS of left-hand side of shirt (see p. 51).

e. stitching interfacing layer of collar to shirt neck edge

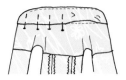

f. pinning unsewn edge of collar over neckline seam stitches

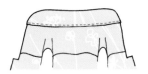

g. edgestitching along collar neck seam

h. sewing cuff onto sleeve along sleeve hemline

09 t-shirt minidress

You can make up this dress in less than an hour. There are no hems – just cut with pinking shears for super-quick and pretty edges. Sew 4 short seams on your sewing machine, add a few pins, and you have an outfit. Easy!

what you need:

tools:
styling design ruler / pinking shears

materials:
31½ in. (80 cm) jersey fabric
10 in. x 2⅜ in. (25 x 6 cm) piece thin cardboard (plus scissors)
pattern paper

To cut out

To make the pattern

1 Trace FRT NECK SHAPE TEMPLATE (illus. b; page 48) onto cardboard, flipping over the cardboard at CF line to create complete shape. Cut out.

2 Draw a rectangle:

size 6–8: 17¾ x 30¾ in. (45 x 78 cm);

size 10–12: 19¼ x 30¾ in. (49 x 78 cm) (illus. a).

3 Draw the CF & CB line lengthwise through the center.

4 Measure 15 in. (38 cm) up from hemline and draw a line across. This is the waistline.

5 To create side seam shaping, on both sides of the rectangle:

a Measure 7 in. (18 cm) down from waistline. Mark a point on side line. This is the hip point.

b Join this point to a point 1½ in. (4 cm) in at the waistline (for waist shaping).

c Draw a line up vertically 8¾ in. (22 cm) from waistline. Mark a notch here. This is the underarm point.

d Continue up to a point 2 in. (5 cm) in at the shoulder line.

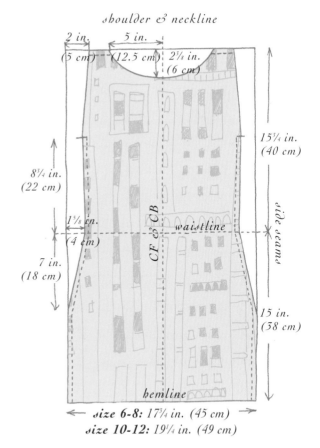

shoulder & neckline

2 in. (5 cm) 5 in. (12.5 cm) 2⅜ in. (6 cm)

15¼ in. (40 cm)

8¾ in. (22 cm)

1⅝ in. (4 cm)

CF & CB

waistline

side seam

7 in. (18 cm)

15 in. (38 cm)

hemline

← *size 6-8:* 17¼ in. (45 cm) →
size 10-12: 19¼ in. (49 cm)

a. making the paper pattern

6 To create front neck shaping (leave the back as a straight line):

a On the shoulder and neckline, mark points with notches on either side of the CF line 5 in. (12.5 cm) across. These are SNPs.

b Join these points with a curve using the FRT NECK SHAPE TEMPLATE.

7 Cut out paper pattern leaving shoulder and neck as a straight line but with front neck shape drawn onto pattern.

To cut out

1 On double layer of fabric cut out dress using pinking shears. Snip notches (SNP and underarm).

2 On one layer of fabric only, position FRT NECK SHAPE TEMPLATE between SNP notches and mark shape on fabric.

3 Cut out with pinking shears.

To make the dress

1 Sew side seams from underarm notches to hemline.

2 Sew shoulder seams from SNP.

3 Turn dress RS out.

5 in. (12.5 cm)

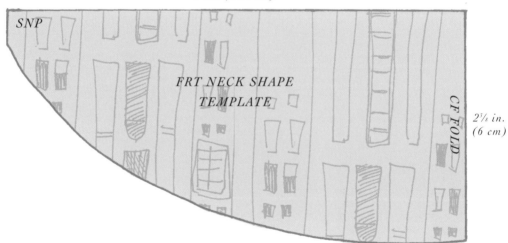

SNP

FRT NECK SHAPE TEMPLATE

CF FOLD

2⅛ in. (6 cm)

b. front neck shape template at 100%

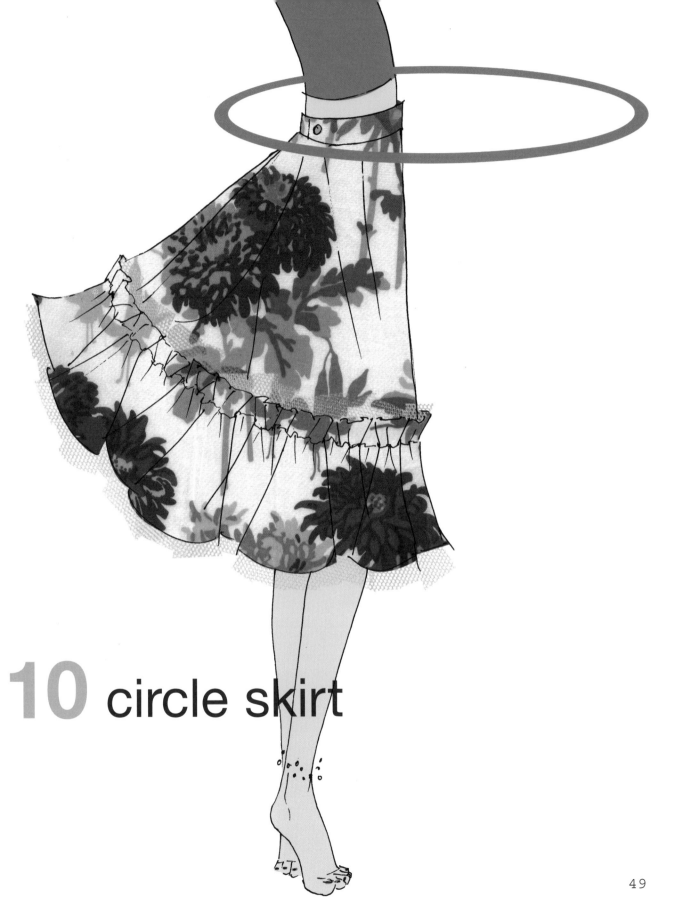

10 circle skirt

*S*ummer – garden parties, cherries, walks in the park...For times like these, a girl needs something pretty to have fun in. With a full shape, waistband, and flash of net petticoat, this is a skirt to enjoy summer in. And it looks great when you twirl!

To cut out

For the skirt

1 From top left-hand corner of your pattern paper draw a 20 in. (50 cm) horizontal line and a 20 in. (50 cm) vertical line.
2 Draw an arc from the left corner with a 20 in. (50 cm) radius, using a piece of string attached to a pencil (illus. a).
3 Draw another arc from same corner point with radius according to your size:
size 6–8: 4⅜ in. (11 cm);
size 10–12: 4¾ in. (12 cm).
4 Mark a notch 8¼ in. (21 cm) from radius of small arc along horizontal line. This is the zipper position notch.
5 Label vertical line CF & CB FOLD.
6 Cut out pattern and label it FRT & BK CIRCLE SKIRT – CUT 2 ON FOLD (illus. b).

For the hem ruffles

1 From your main fabric cut 8 in. (20 cm) wide strips across the width of the fabric.
If you are using 60 in. (150 cm) wide fabric, cut 4 strips. If you are using 53/45 in. (135/115 cm) wide fabric, cut 5 strips.
2 From the net cut strips as for the fabric but 9 in. (23 cm) wide.

what you need:

tools:
26 in. (65 cm) string
zipper foot

materials:
2½ yd. (220 cm) light-/medium-weight fabric
1⅓ yd. (120 cm) net
8 in. (20 cm) zipper
6 in. (15 cm) interfacing
⅝ in. (1.5 cm)-diameter button
pattern paper

For the waistband

Cut 2 rectangles, 1 in fabric and 1 in interfacing:
size 6–8: 3¼ x 30 in. (8 x 76 cm);
size 10–12: 3¼ x 33 in. (8 x 84 cm).
Mark notches on both sides of rectangle 1½ in. (4 cm) from one end, to indicate the waistband extension.

To make the circle skirt

1 Join FRT and BK SKIRT pieces on 1 side seam from zipper position notch to hem.
2 Follow instructions for inserting the zipper for Pencil Skirt on page 29.
3 Sew other side seam.
4 Follow instructions for preparing and attaching waistband on page 30.

To make & attach the fabric and net ruffles

1 Sew together ends of fabric strips, making a very long loop.
2 Turn top and bottom edges of fabric ruffle under by ⅜ in. (1 cm) and sew.
3 Fold ruffle into quarters and mark quarter points with straight pins.
4 Using a loose basting stitch, sew a line of stitches 1 in. (2.5 cm) down from 1 edge, between 2 pins. Gather fabric between 2 quarter-point marks so that this section of ruffle ends up measuring 30⅜ in. (77 cm). Repeat for other 3 sections of ruffle.
5 Sew along gathering line to secure gathering in place.
6 Remove basting stitches.
7 Follow above procedure for net ruffle, but do not hem edges.
8 Sew through net ruffle and fabric ruffle at gathered stitchlines, with net underneath, to join.
9 Lay ruffle on top of skirt with gathered stitchline positioned ⅜ in. (1.5 cm) up from bottom edge of skirt, and pin.
10 Sew through gathered stitchline to attach ruffle to skirt.

To make the buttonhole

1 Mark a buttonhole position in center of waistband, to left of zipper and ⅜ in. (1.5 cm) from end.
2 Sew a ⅜ in. (1.5 cm) buttonhole, using the buttonhole function on your sewing machine.
3 Mark position of button with a straight pin against right-hand end of buttonhole, pushing pin through to waistband extension underneath. Sew button on at this point.

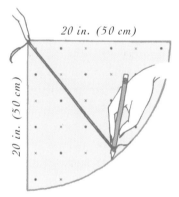

20 in. (50 cm)

20 in. (50 cm)

a. drawing the pattern

FRT & BK
CIRCLE SKIRT
CUT 2 ON FOLD

CF & CB FOLD

b. labeling the pattern

11 headband

Curly hair, straight hair, blonde, black, or red...whatever you have, some days you need a change. Quick and easy to make, this headband uses two different fabrics, so it's reversible. Choose the fabric to match your mood – it's easier than changing your hair color!

what you need:

tools:
styling design ruler

materials:
2 x 4 in. (10 cm) light-/medium-weight fabric
4 in. (10 cm) of ³/₄ in. (2 cm) wide elastic
pattern paper

To cut out

1 Draw a rectangle 19 x 3 in. (48 x 8 cm).
2 3 in. (8 cm) in from ends of rectangle, taper band in by ³/₄ in. (2 cm) on either side (illus. a).
3 Cut HEADBAND in 2 different fabrics.

To make the headband

1 With RS together, join 2 HEADBAND pieces together along length edges. Trim SA to ¼ in. (5 mm).
2 Turn RS out. Press flat.
3 Turn raw ends under ⅜ in. (1 cm).
4 Thread elastic ends ⅜ in. (1 cm) into open ends of headband. Pin elastic ends in place.
5 Edgestitch headband ends to attach elastic (illus. b).

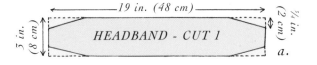

HEADBAND - CUT 1
— 19 in. (48 cm) —
3 in. (8 cm)
³/₄ in. (2 cm)
a.

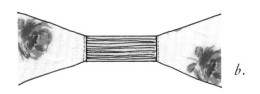

b.

12 circular bag

This is a sweet little handbag – good for day, great for night. We made it in a cute upholstery fabric, with a contrasting zipper and sparkly pink piping. In a rush to make the party? Forget the piping and go!

To cut out

FT & BK BAG: 4⅜ in. (11 cm) radius circle – CUT 2
Fold into eighths and mark notches at these intervals (illus. a; page 56).
BOTTOM STRIP: 16 x 2⅜ in. (41 x 6 cm) – CUT 1
Fold in half, mark notches on both sides of strip at 3⅛ in. (7.8 cm) from both sides of center, and notch 3⅛ in. (7.8 cm) out from these notches. Also notch center of each end (illus. b; page 56).

what you need:

tools:
compass
zipper foot
pinking shears

materials:
10 in. (25 cm) heavy-weight woven fabric
19½ in. (50 cm) woven fabric *or* 4 in. (10 cm) stretch knit fabric for piping
10 in. (25 cm) interfacing
10 in. (25 cm) zipper
25½ in. (65 cm) narrow (0 gauge) cording

finished size:
diameter = 8 in. (20 cm)

TOP ZIPPER STRIPS: 10½ x1⅜ in. (26 x 3.5 cm) – CUT 2
Fold in half, mark notch on 1 side, and 3⅛ in. (7.8 cm) out from both sides of center notch (illus. c; page 56).
INTERFACING: Cut all above pieces.
Fuse interfacing to fabric.
HANDLE: 14 x 1¼ in. (35 x 3 cm) – CUT 1
BIAS STRIPS: 25½ x1¼ in. (65 x 3 cm) – CUT 2
(If using woven fabric, cut on bias, see below.)

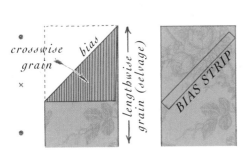

Cutting bias strips

Bias means diagonal to the grain. When fabric is cut on the bias it has more give and so will mold along different-shaped seamlines.
To find the bias, fold the fabric with the lengthwise grain, or selvage, to the crosswise grain. The folded edge is the bias. Draw this folded line with a dressmaker's marking pencil and then you can draw your bias strips on the fabric out from this line.

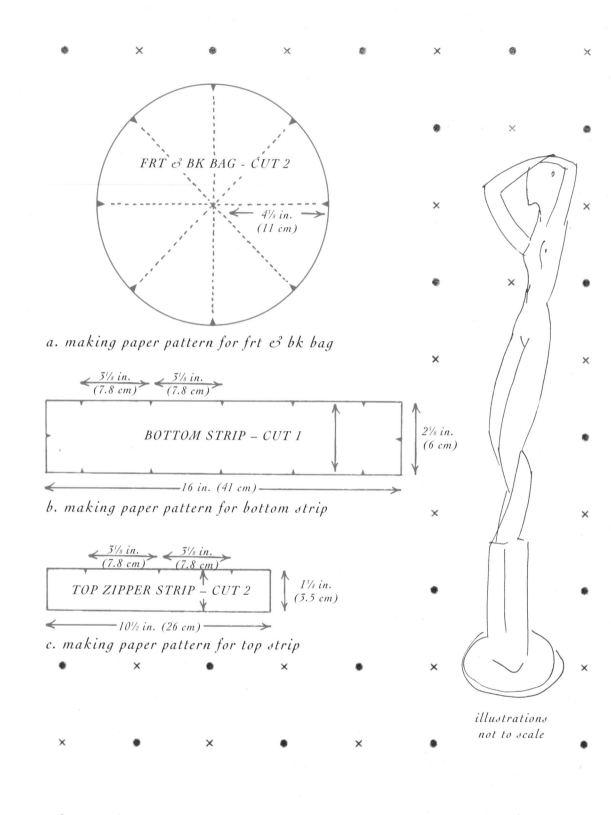

FRT & BK BAG - CUT 2

4⅛ in.
(11 cm)

a. making paper pattern for frt & bk bag

3⅛ in.
(7.8 cm)

3⅛ in.
(7.8 cm)

BOTTOM STRIP – CUT 1

2⅜ in.
(6 cm)

16 in. (41 cm)

b. making paper pattern for bottom strip

3⅛ in.
(7.8 cm)

3⅛ in.
(7.8 cm)

TOP ZIPPER STRIP – CUT 2

1⅜ in.
(3.5 cm)

10½ in. (26 cm)

c. making paper pattern for top strip

*illustrations
not to scale*

To make the bag

To attach the zipper

1 Open zipper. Place facedown onto RS of TOP ZIPPER STRIP, zipper tape edge to unnotched length edge. Secure with straight pins.

2 Using zipper foot, sew along seamline. When you come to the zipper pull tab, leaving the needle down through the fabric, lift the zipper foot. With needle down, pull tab to close zipper. Lower foot, continue sewing to end of zipper tape (illus. d).

3 Repeat to sew other side of zipper to second top zipper strip.

4 Edgestitch on RS fabric (illus. e).

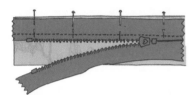

d. attaching the zipper

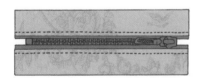

e. edgestitching

To make the handle

1 Using the pinking shears, trim along 1 length edge of HANDLE.

2 Fold lengthwise into a third, with RS out and pinked edge lying on top. Pin perpendicularly. Zigzag through center along length to make handle.

3 Position ends of handle together on end notch of BOTTOM STRIP. Sew in place inside of seamline (illus. f).

4 Sew end of bottom strip without handle to base of zipper end of TOP ZIPPER STRIP. Edgestitch on bottom strip, with all SA pushed toward bottom strip (illus. f).

f. securing the handle

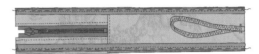

g. attaching the piping

To attach the piping

1 Lay cording lengthwise in center of WS of BIAS STRIP. Fold strip in half to encase cording. Pin.

2 Using zipper foot, sew along length of BIAS STRIP, as close to the encased cording as possible, to make piping.

3 Place piping lengthwise along RS-up seamlines of bottom strip and top zipper strip. Baste inside of seamlines to secure.

4 Repeat to attach piping to opposite side of bottom strip and zipper strip (illus. g).

To attach the front & back panels

1 With zipper open, use standard presser foot to sew ends of bottom strip and top zipper strips together, sewing through piping, handle, and zipper tape.

2 Edgestitch bottom strip, with all SA pushed toward bottom strip.

3 With RS together, match one notch of FRT BAG circle to middle notch of bottom strip. Using this as the starting point, pin frt bag circle to bottom strip, matching notches.

4 Using zipper foot, baste bottom strip to frt bag circle inside of seamline.

5 Go around again, using shorter straight stitch length, as close to piping cording as possible.

6 Attach BK BAG in same way.

7 Using the pinking shears, trim seams. Turn bag RS out.

*Put on a bow -
& let's go dancing...*

13 bows

A cute bow goes a long way. These little pins are as easy as pie to make and great for using up fabric scraps or short lengths of silk ribbon. Pin onto your cocktail dress, leather jacket, ballet flats, or hair clip. Do not pin onto your little sister!

To cut out

large bow
BOW LOOP: 5½ x 10¼ in. (14 x 26 cm) – CUT 1
CENTER TIE: 2⅜ x 4 in. (6 x 10 cm) – CUT 1

small bow
BOW LOOP: 3½ x 6¾ in. (9 x 17 cm) – CUT 1
CENTER TIE: 2 x 2⅜ in. (5 x 6 cm) – CUT 1

ribbon bow
BOW LOOP: 6¾ in. (17 cm) of 1 in. (2.5 cm) wide ribbon – CUT 1
CENTER TIE: 1¼ in. (3 cm) of ⅝ in. (1.5 cm) wide ribbon – CUT 1

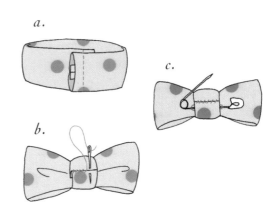

To make the bows

To make bow loops
1 Fold fabric in half lengthwise, RS together. Sew along seamline to form a tube.
2 Attach a large safety pin to one end of the tube. Push it through the tube to turn tube RS out.
3 Join 2 ends together by placing one seamline on top of the other. Sew through both seamlines.
4 Trim SA to ¼ in. (5 mm) (illus. a).

To make center tie
1 Fold fabric in half lengthwise, RS together. Sew SA along seamline to form a tube.
2 Turn RS out, following instructions in step 2 of "To make bow loops."

3 Wrap CENTER TIE around middle of bow loop, with center tie join at the back and join of bow loop covered. Turn end of center tie that lies on top under. Overstitch to secure (illus. b).

To attach safety pin
With safety pin open, thread head end under center tie at back of bow. Wrap thread around pin a few times and stitch pin onto edge of center tie to hold pin in place (illus. c).

For bows made with ribbon, follow instructions in "To make bow loops" and "To make center tie" from step 3 in both sections and then attach safety pin.

14 puppy dog

$\mathcal{O}$h puppy love! This adorable doggy is easy to make and easy to love. We used an upholstery fabric for his body and lined his ears with a contrasting floral fabric. Pick out some cute buttons for eyes. Perfect for a baby, or better still, for sitting pretty on your sofa.

To cut out

Copy scaled pattern pieces (see page 63) onto pattern paper. Each square = 1 in. (2.5 cm). Cut double layer of fabric.

To make the doggy

To make the ears

1 With RS of 1 main fabric DOGGY EAR and 1 lining fabric DOGGY EAR together, sew around outer curved edge. Repeat for 2nd ear.
2 Trim SA to ¼ in. (5 mm) and turn RS out. Press flat.
3 Place ears together with main fabrics together, lining on the outside. Baste ears together along top open edge inside of seamline.
4 Place ears on RS of 1 DOGGY BODY piece between ear position notches, matching A and B.
5 Sew ears in position with correct SA.

To make the body

1 Sew buttons onto each DOGGY BODY at eye positioning mark.
2 With RS of 2 DOGGY BODY pieces together, sew from C along top of the nose to the first opening notch, then from the 2nd opening notch to D.

3 Sew DOGGY UNDERBELLY pieces together along central belly seam.

4 Sew DOGGY CHIN to underbelly section, matching seams marked E.

5 Join underbelly section to main body, matching C to C and D to D. First sew one side C to D, then the other side.

6 Trim SA to ¼ in. (5 mm) and clip around curves up to but not through stitching.

7 Turn RS out. Stuff body firmly with polyester fiber filling in the following order: tail, legs, bottom, nose, lower body, and then upper body.

8 Close opening using even slipstitch.

To make the collar

1 Fold the ⅛ in. (3 mm) wide ribbon in half to make a loop. Place it on 1 HEART TAG piece, with ends three-quarters of the way down from the top of the heart shape.

2 Using fabric adhesive, glue 2 layers of heart tag together, with ribbon loop ends sandwiched between.

3 When adhesive is dry, thread ⅝ in. (1.5 cm) wide ribbon through heart tag loop and wrap it around neck of the dog. Cut to size, leaving enough to overlap the ribbon. Turn one end of ribbon under and hand-stitch the ribbon down under the chin.

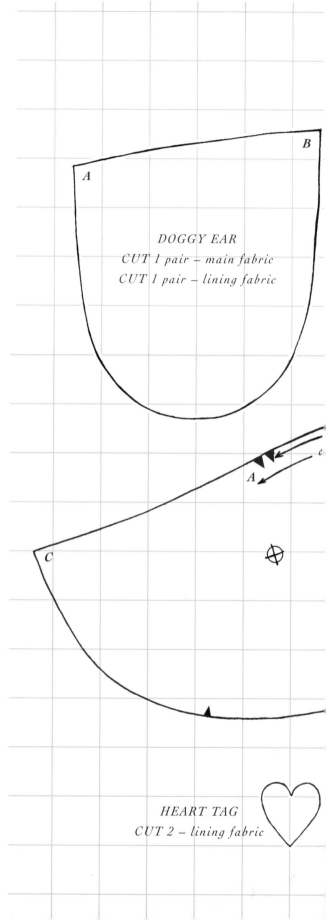

A   *B*

DOGGY EAR
CUT 1 pair – main fabric
CUT 1 pair – lining fabric

e

A

C

HEART TAG
CUT 2 – lining fabric

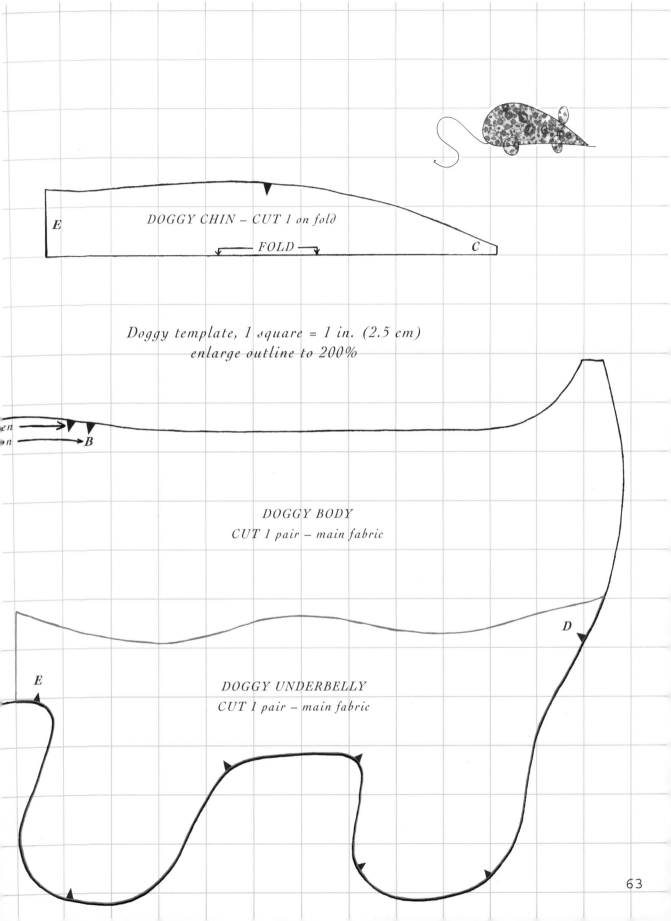

DOGGY CHIN – CUT 1 on fold

E

FOLD

C

Doggy template, 1 square = 1 in. (2.5 cm)
enlarge outline to 200%

en

n → B

DOGGY BODY
CUT 1 pair – main fabric

D

E

DOGGY UNDERBELLY
CUT 1 pair – main fabric

Many thanks to: Catie Ziller for her original idea
& the opportunity to create things; Leanne Finn-Davies
for making beautiful clothes & writing concise
instructions; Kathy Steer for her hard work & rescuing
files; Ben, Ruth, & Amelia for the photos;
Tris for the camera; & ...

*... Stu, Gracie, & Pops,
for lots of helping ...*

First published in the United States in 2007 by
Watson-Guptill Publications
Nielsen Business Media,
a division of The Nielsen Company
770 Broadway, New York, NY 10003
www.watsonguptill.com

Library of Congress Control Number: 2007929712

ISBN-10: 0-8230-9958-X
ISBN-13: 978-0-8230-9958-0

First published in France by Marabout
(Hachette Livre) in 2007
© 2007 Marabout (Hachette Livre)

Printed in China

First printing, 2007

1 2 3 4 5 6 7 8 / 14 13 12 11 10 09 08 07

... & for lovely drawings.
xxx

for John Calvey
1917-2006